SOCIAL CITIZENS

A POSITIVE APPROACH TO SOCIAL MEDIA & PARENTING IN A DIGITAL WORLD

Nancy Smith

DEDICATION

To my son, Evan. I am so proud of you and am excited for your bright future. To my husband, Stewart. Thank you for believing in me and for encouraging me to pursue my dreams.

CONTENTS

INTRODUCTION

My decision to become an advocate for social media began after a parent session at my son's school that was supposed to deal with online safety. The session, however, was focused on all of the dangers of social media. While the information presented was indeed technically true, I found the whole approach to be overly biased and extreme. At the end of the parent session, we were all left with many frightening examples of cyber-bullying, sexting, and child pornography. I thought the session lacked any positive direction or guidance on how to help our kids use social media responsibly, other than to completely discourage our kids from using it.

I went home and discussed the session with my husband. I realize that though the session was positioned as an online safety session, I wanted parents to understand how kids can use all the exciting, emerging technology to their advantage—rather than discourage its use altogether. We live in a time of incredible opportunity for creating connections and learning with these powerful resources at our fingertips. Clearly, I'm not an advocate for not allowing technology use and cutting it off. At the session, the presenter's advice seemed unrealistic to me about how parents should handle their kids using it.

After posting my frustrations to Facebook, dozens of friends joined in the conversation. It quickly became clear that this was a shared issue. As the solution I was looking for wasn't out there, and my dissatisfaction with what was available, I was inspired to initiate a movement and to build a hub of practical advice that parents were looking for and one that kids need.

> *I believe what we can do better together is to talk about our experiences. What works, what doesn't—in an environment free from fear mongering, shame, and judgement.*

My belief that social media can be a positive experience is not based in an idealist version of reality. It's something I work toward every day. My 12 year career in digital marketing and social media has included working with brands like Travel Alberta, Sport Chek, and Samsung by helping them utilize social media and connect them with their consumers online. Now, I do the same thing with families; helping adults discover the positive aspects of social media and working with kids on how they can be responsible social citizens in this rapidly changing digital environment.

I currently teach people about social media and digital marketing at Mount Royal University, the University of Calgary, Bow Valley College, and the Canadian Marketing Association. I have been speaking about this topic for over 10 years, building my platform, using my voice and providing practical workshops and sessions at large-scale conferences. I'm very much a part of the conversation on the perils related to social media, but I'm not a doomsayer. I talk about what's not working and I equip people with the right tools to go forth and navigate based on improved knowledge, confidence, and peace of mind. Technology is everywhere, it can't be avoided, and it absolutely can be used for good.

I'm also a mom to a teen, and while I'm scared at times, I'm also thrilled at the options and access we have to make global impacts and I believe in focusing on that. It's my mission to provide families with the right support and tools to help us become the best well-rounded social citizens we can be. Because, when we are, we shape a better world full of hope and possibility—showcasing the true potential of positive social connectedness.

I use the internet every day for work and for my own personal use. I enjoy connecting with friends and family on Facebook. I use Twitter to learn new things from authors and thought leaders I like and admire, and stay current on news and what is happening in the world. I love to scroll through the images in my Instagram feed and escape my everyday routine via the escapism of viewing beautiful photos of destinations around the world. I watch YouTube videos to learn how to do things and to be entertained. I love social media. I love the opportunities to learn and to connect with people online. And I love to teach and help people make sense of this digital world.

That is why I decided to write this book, and to create the resource hub, SocialCitizens.ca. I find something new to learn and to adapt to every day. I love the challenge of interpreting how technology and social media are being used and to help people, including parents like you, understand it all. I also want to help kids figure out the best ways to navigate through the challenges and opportunities that the internet and social media present to them.

This book is intended to be a positive resource for social media use. If you are looking for a book that condemns the use of digital technologies for kids under 18, or one that will frighten you with statistics or stories of the worst cases of crime that can happen, this is not the right resource for you. The goal of this book is to help you establish a set of informed guidelines that you can use to make sense of the technology you can use in your family. These guidelines need to be appropriate for your values, as well as for the age and maturity of your children. Here, I will offer you recommendations of how you can embrace technology and develop a healthy, balanced approach. I want to share an approach where we can embrace technology it and determine how we will allow it in our family's lives vs. allowing it to control our lives.

If you are willing to be open-minded, I believe you can help guide your kids on how to use social media safely, responsibly, and respect-fully. Throughout the chapters in this book I will help you understand how our kids are using technology and social media, and I will share the positive benefits and opportunities available.

My hope is that after you read this book, you will feel empowered and not overwhelmed. I also hope that you will be further inspired to learning more about this ever-changing digital and social media world. In addition, I invite you to continue our learning together. I aim to be a helpful resource for you. You can "like" my Facebook page facebook.com/socialcitizens where we engage in healthy discussions and are free of judgement from asking questions, or visit my web-site socialcitizens.ca to continue your learning. Let's share and learn together as a community.

CHAPTER 1

TECHNOLOGY, SOCIAL MEDIA, AND HOW KIDS USE IT

t's easy to understand why parents are concerned about technology. The amount of time kids spend using their smartphones, computers, and playing video games seems to increase every year. Indeed, it's likely that this is one of the reasons why you are reading this book.

I have found it very challenging to find credible and balanced information in my quest for more information that will help guide the decisions for what is right for my family. It seems like there are new stories about extreme examples of what can go wrong if we let our kids use technology being shared almost daily. I recently saw a video from a business author that I like and admire as he was interviewed by a parenting expert. He stated that parents are raising kids that are that chemically addicted to technology and compared it to how most alcoholics discover alcohol when they are teens. I was shocked at the comparison—and that he didn't state that chemical addition "could" happen—he presented it is a reality for teens that use social media. Obviously, this was as alarming to me as I am sure it was to the other viewers of that video.

As a mom to a teen, I am scared at times, just like you might be when you see videos like that. But as someone who works in the field of digital marketing and social media as my profession, I am also thrilled at the options and access to technology we now have available to us. It frustrates me when I see videos like the one I described above make headlines and dominate the conversations of parenting experts. However, I have found it really challenging to find resources that share my interest in providing a credible source of information, especially one that has a balanced perspective rather than just spouting doom and gloom.

I believe that the more information we have to learn about technology and the online world, the more we are empowered to make the right choices for our kids and ourselves. But it seems like what is lacking in the headlines, is information about the positive aspects of technology. I am committed to seeking more positive resources for my own parenting, and I want to take this opportunity to share them with you as well.

Balance & Moderation

Here is an example of a recent study that supports my belief that there are positive aspects to our kids using technology. In 2017, a University of Oxford study of 120,000 15 year olds was released in which there was a positive correlation between the amount of screen time and wellbeing. The researchers found that time spent on technology may enhance communication skills, creativity, and knowledge, and they further concluded that some previous research oversimplified the relationship between the mental wellbeing of kids and screen time.

The key is ensuring balance and moderation in technology use. The study suggests that the amount of time teens can spend on computers each day before harming their wellbeing is 257 minutes (4 hours and 17 minutes). The research stated that unless devices are overused or interfere with school or activities, that digital technology may have advantages for kids in a connected world.

Trust me, I am not setting a daily timer for 257 minutes in our home! However, when I think about how my son uses his devices, he probably averages about that much screen time. Note that I say, averages, because I know some days are less and on occasion he spends more time. He typically watches YouTube videos right after coming home from school for about an hour before he does his homework. After dinner, if he doesn't head to the gym with his buddies, he might play some Xbox for an hour or go online again and watch more YouTube. Closer to bedtime, he usually reads a book, with no devices used in his bedroom. This is how we manage to create balance and find moderation in our home.

I myself sometimes find it really difficult to resist the urge to check my phone to see what's new on Facebook, or to check the latest update on LinkedIn, so I understand the challenge of self-control my son faces. Plus, many popular sites and apps we use are programmed with features like notifications that compel us to frequently check in and not feel like we are going to miss anything. I have had to turn off all notifications on Facebook, Twitter, Instagram, and LinkedIn on both my smartphone and laptop so that I can control and manage the time I use these apps. This practice has really improved my focus and attention on tasks, and has cut down on the overall time I would consider as wasted.

The 80/20 Rule

I often refer to the Pareto Principle as a guideline that I follow in many of my actions as a parent, as well as in my personal life. The basic idea of the Pareto Principle is that most things in life are not distributed evenly, with some contributing more than others. It is more commonly referred to as the 80/20 rule. Here is how I apply this principle to my positive approach on social media use and parenting.

Most people worry excessively about the worst that could happen to their kids online, and thus tend to obsess about internet safety and the need to police what their kids are doing. I know of parents who use apps that monitor every text and app their kids access and every video they watch on YouTube. When I ask if they have encountered anything to be concerned about, the response is typically "not yet".

In my opinion, this is an example of the 80/20 Pareto Principle in parenting.

As a parent, if you spend most of your time trying to monitor and react to what your child is doing online, you are wasting precious time. If you only read the negative headlines that are a mainstay in the media about the evils of technology, you are unbalanced in your approach. Instead, I believe that shifting your energy and awareness to being proactive about how you teach and guide your child to use social media and technology safely and responsibly is a more effective way to deal with the ever-changing digital landscape.

Note that I am not saying you do not need to be aware of the dangers that exist online. These are very real, and should definitely be a part of your ongoing search for new information about what you need to be aware of. Later, in Chapter 6, I will provide you with some warning signs and behaviour that will help you. However, if we focus 20% of our time on this endeavour—rather than 80%—I believe you will experience powerful shifts in understanding the role of technology in your teen's life.

My goal is to provide you with the positive side of the story, in order to help you establish a balance that is right for you and your family.

Understanding Social Media

If you understand what your child is doing online, you will have an understanding of why the attraction for them to use it is so strong. In fact, if you yourself use social media such as Facebook, YouTube, or Twitter, you might be surprised to learn that how kids use social media isn't all that different from how you do. The apps they use might be different, but the way they use it doesn't differ that much.

Let's start with a definition of what social media is. In its most basic form, social media can be defined as people connecting to other people using technology. That's it. Some popular social media apps for teens include Instagram, Snapchat, and YouTube. However, new social media apps and popular sites emerge all of the time, so it is a good idea to ask your child what sites they use the most. In Chapter 5, I will give you some advice on how you can talk with your child and learn more about the sites and apps they are using. In the meantime, if you want to get a better understanding and an overview of each of these social media sites (and many others) I recommend you check out the website commonsensemedia.org, where they provide easy to understand reviews.

Where it might start to get confusing is the range of social media sites and networks that exist. It can be overwhelming to try to keep up with all of the options available. As such, I would recommend that you don't focus all your energy on trying, instead, it is better to focus on the one(s) you are going to allow your child to use.

While many different social media apps exist, the way that kids actually use them is in one of these three ways:

1. Connect: with friends via messaging and comments on posts
2. Share: photos and videos that express their views and personality
3. Entertainment: play games, and find funny and entertaining content

For teens, most use social media to stay connected with their friends. Friendships are very important for the healthy development of social skills and self-confidence. Plus, most kids typically spend more time with their friends than they do their family! It makes sense that teens use technology and social media to extend the amount of time they get to spend with their friends. When I was a teen, the minute I came home from school, I was busy calling my best friends, and would often spend hours on the telephone sharing stories of what happened that day and planning for the next time we would get to spend together. I am sure my parents were frustrated with the amount of time I spent on the phone, but they also allowed me (within limit) to do this, as it was a part of developing healthy friendships.

Using social media is now one of the most popular ways for teens to stay connected with their friends. There are many different apps that allow them to share with their friends online, and most don't use standard text messaging (SMS) through your cell provider—like you probably do. Direct messaging, or DMing, is a way to send private messages to a friend or a group of friends. For example, lots of kids use Instagram and Snapchat mainly for the private messaging capabilities rather than the functionality of sharing content with their followers.

What are They Doing Online?

One of the biggest concerns I hear from parents is that they fear their kids are wasting time online and spending too much time connected to their devices. "What are they doing and watching?" The best way for you to get the answer to this question is to ask your child. Let them explain what they like to do and why they like to watch the videos that they do online. It is really important that if you are prepared to ask this, that you must also be prepared to be very open-minded and not dismiss what their answers are. Don't be judgmental.

Recently, a friend of mine shared on Facebook that their 8 year old wanted to show her a video that they thought was so cool on YouTube. Much to her surprise and delight, it was a music video by The Piano Guys playing *Let it Go* (Disney's Frozen) *Vivaldi's Winter*. If you haven't seen a video of the Piano Guys, you should check them out. They are two talented musicians, one is a pianist and the other plays cello. Together they have over 5 million subscribers on YouTube, and their videos have been viewed over 1 billion times. Needless to say, I think she was pleased to learn something new about her child and that he loved that kind of music.

Don't assume the worst. I am a firm believer that children are essentially good and for the most part will use the internet responsibly. Of course, they will make mistakes, just like you did when you were their age.

Still, you might want to prepare yourself to see some things that you don't understand. Let me give you an example: a few years ago my son was really into playing the game Minecraft on our Xbox gaming system. The simplest way for me to describe what this game is, in case you are not familiar, is that Minecraft is a game where you mine and build different 3D blocks in a virtual world. It's kind of like an online version of Lego. If you search Minecraft videos on YouTube, you will find millions of videos of people playing the game online. Currently, *Minecraft* is the second-most searched term on YouTube. Considering that YouTube is the second largest search engine in the world next to their parent company Google, this is a testament to the popularity of the game.

I tried watching a few of the videos he loved and, to be honest, I found it really boring. I couldn't understand why he would want to watch someone else playing the game instead of playing it himself. Sometimes, he would be watching videos of other people playing the game on the iPad, while also playing it at the same time. (Remember, no judgement or parent shaming please.)

When I asked why, he explained that he wanted to get better at the game and learned new skills from watching other people do it. He also said some of the videos were funny and entertaining. He thought it was pretty cool when he left a comment on one of the videos, that the popular YouTuber responded and thanked him.

Times have changed in our household and, although my son no longer watches Minecraft videos or plays that game anymore, he continues to watch videos on YouTube. In fact, he watches more videos online than he watches television. Now, his video feed is filled with sports highlights and his basketball heroes. I know this because one of the rules in our house is that I can regularly check his viewing history at any time. We also ensure that he is watching videos while in the main living areas of our home, so we can randomly see what he is watching. These are important checkpoints that you should consider implementing for your peace of mind, and for their online safety.

In most cases, kids tend to start using technology and devices to play games and for entertainment. It usually isn't until middle school when they start to use their devices for communicating with friends.

Although it seems like the time when kids start going online is getting younger with each year that passes. This might be because more parents are letting their children get phones at a younger age.

What is the Right Age for a Smartphone?

This is a new rite of passage for kids today, and many parents have the question: "How old should my child be before I give them a smartphone?" I am not going to give you one age as the right answer, because I don't believe there is one magical age to be the perfect time.

I think it is important for families to assess their unique situation and then make a decision based on their individual child. There are many factors for you to consider when making this decision. For example:

- Assess why your child feels they need a smartphone (it's usually the child asking for one long before the parents are ready!). Is it a want, or is it a need? An example of the need for a phone is a child who walks to school and may be involved in afterschool activities. As a parent, you may need to have a device to get in contact with your child to communicate plans, etc. Be careful not to let peer influence determine when to get a phone for your child. Wanting one because their friends have one may not be the best answer to determine the timing for giving them a phone.
- How mature is your child? Some families may have a 12 year old who is more mature than a child that is older. With maturity, children tend to have a greater understanding of responsibility. If you give a child a phone and they are not mature enough for the responsibilities of owning a device, you could be setting them up for making poor decisions.
- Is your child responsible for taking care of their belongings? Smartphones are expensive devices and, if lost, damaged, or stolen, it is very costly to replace. Because there will be a significant cost for replacement, it is a good idea to discuss the cost of the device, whether or not it is a new phone or one that is being handed down to them. Be clear about how much it costs each

month for data, as well as how much it costs to replace a screen if it is cracked or broken. It is important to be transparent that you are investing in their privilege to use a device.

- What technology is your child already using? Do they use, or have regular access to, tablets, gaming devices and systems, and computers? Have they respected your rules for use of these technologies? Their use here would be a good indication to determine if they will respect your limits for using a phone.
- What are your family values regarding technology and its use? How do you as a parent use a smartphone? Remember, our kids model our behaviour, so it is important to be aware of what they see us do with our devices.

For my family, our son was 10 years old when we decided to give him a phone. I was a working mom and he took the school bus for transportation to school. We decided to give him one of my old devices so that we could easily communicate about where each other was. It gave me peace of mind knowing I could contact him and he could easily reach me. He has now been using a phone for over two years, and has been very responsible with the device and his use.

If you make the decision to provide your child with a phone, the desire to talk with their friends online will likely follow. It is highly unlikely, however, that they will use the actual "phone" feature to call anyone other than their parents. Instead, kids prefer to use messaging apps. At the time I wrote this book, the two most popular social media apps for messaging were Snapchat and Instagram, but there are many others. This use is likely quite different from how you typically use your device, so be prepared for a bit of a learning curve. I provide some examples in Chapter 3 about how you can approach learning about how your child and their friends use technology.

Guidelines for Your Family

How can you best support your tween/teen with technology and social media? If you decide to allow your child to use social media it is important to establish some guidelines regarding what is right for your family. I suggest you focus on what matters to you most, then make a list of clear expectations for use.

For my family, we focus on:

- Time: we allow him to use technology for up to 3 hours outside of the time he may use technology for homework. We are teaching him how to manage his time as effectively as he can, both online and offline.
- Place: his device is not allowed to be used in his bedroom. He uses his smartphone in our living room on the main floor of our home. It is also clear that he must follow the rules of his school and sporting teams regarding when he can and can't use his smartphone.
- Content: our son knows he cannot download any apps without our permission. We then have all of the passwords to accounts we allow him to use. We perform random checks to ensure that he is using his device safely and responsibly.

We also do our best to model being responsible and good social citizens so that we are "walking the talk". Most importantly, we have frequent discussions about social media and stories and content we see online. Our goal is to ensure our son is comfortable discussing what he sees online with us, and that he is not hiding things.

When we demonstrate healthy habits and provide our kids with clear boundaries for using digital technology and social media we are creating a solid foundation for its use.

CHAPTER 2

PARENTING IN THIS DIGITAL AGE

This is not a parenting book. Nor is this a book of rules on how to manage your kids' smartphones or social media use. Instead, my hope is to provide you with insights and perspectives to help you evolve your parenting in an area you may be less familiar with. You can either take my advice directly, or you can use it as a guideline to help you figure out what will work best for your family.

New Parenting Challenges

We are the first generation of parents who are navigating how our kids use social media and technology in their daily lives. We don't have the benefit of years of proven research from previous generations on the effects our actions will have on their physical and mental development. We can't ask our parents how they handled decisions about what apps they let us use, or what was the right age to let us get our first cell phone. The challenges we now face as parents are new, and can be overwhelming.

It is easy to be concerned about how much time your kids spend online texting, gaming, and on social media. I would, however, suggest that these concerns could be compared to the ones parents of other generations have had to manage. In fact, if asked parents with older children about the challenges they faced regarding their kids and new technology, you would hear answers like: "I think our son is spending too much time playing video games", or "our daughter seems to watch too much mindless television". The similarities that these problems have with regards to our challenges today are that we are all concerned about the wellbeing of our children and that we want the best for them. You might also want the same result that I hope my son has in life: to grow up to be happy, healthy, fulfilled, and able to handle life with confidence and empathy for others.

Navigating how our kids use digital technology and social media is new for all of us. No matter how comfortable you are with technology, we are all in the same place of having to decide what is right for our family. I find that this is where things start to get into "grey" areas in discussions with parents, and it seems like there is a very broad spectrum of acceptance of technology. For example, some parents are strongly against devices being used at all, whereas others are more open to allowing their children to use technology such as tablets, smartphones, and gaming systems. Social media use is no different, and the broad range varies from parents who follow all their kids' online activities on apps like Instagram to others who have banned the use of apps entirely. The key is that you need to decide what is right for your family. Don't base your decisions on what other parents allow or do not. You need to be comfortable with the choices you make.

I also get that it doesn't seem long ago when your biggest concern was: "Should I let my son watch Toy Story one more time, even if it is for the third time in the last 24 hours?" Now we are faced with new technology challenges, like what is the right age to get him a cell phone, and when do I allow him to use social media?

As one parent said to me: "I am most afraid that I don't know what I don't know."

What is Your Relationship with Technology?

So where do we start? Knowing how you feel about technology is a good place to begin. This will help you understand how you want to parent and to make decisions for your kids.

You may not understand all the latest trends and apps in technology, but don't underestimate the value you have in your experience of handling real-life situations. You might get frustrated with not easily understanding all of the technology and social media sites, but I want to stress that you don't need to be an expert. Try to be open-minded about the benefits of using technology in your daily life. As with anything, balance and moderation are essential.

I remember the day my parents bought me a computer. I was 12 years old in Grade 7. My mom worked as an administrative assistant in an engineering company and was using computers at work, which was very progressive for most workplaces in the 1980's. I give her a lot of credit for being ahead of the times as an early adapter. With no internet or computer programs available, however, that first computer couldn't do much more than act as a glorified typewriter. My favourite thing to do was to play a "learn how to type" game, and after hours of practice I became a QWERTY two-handed typing master! (No single-handed hunt-and-peck typing for me!) For fun, my older brothers and I would have competitions to see who could type the most accurately and quickest. To this day, I am the fastest and most accurate typist in my family—and yes, I am still proud of that accomplishment!

My ability to type quickly became very handy when I was entered university. In the early 1990's, we were required to submit our assignments typewritten, and while most students struggled with electronic typewriters or paid someone to type their assignments, I was able to do my own typing on the laptop in my home. This ultimately saved me time and money, which are important resources that people like to save, especially university students.

My parents recognized that technology was changing and that the ability to master typing as a skill would be beneficial in my academic and professional life. In fact, I could assume they recognized that this was a life skill, not unlike needing to teach me how to go to the bank and deposit money into my savings account. Yes, I am old enough that I used to have to line up with my parents in our branch, during banking hours that closed at 4 pm, and waited with others until our turn came and the bank teller could finally help us. My parents set me up for success, and I believe that background in becoming familiar with technology at a young age has helped me be open-minded and adaptable to the ever-evolving digital technology we have today.

The Benefits of Technology

Our homes and workplaces—even our cars—have computers that make our daily lives easier and more efficient. Times are different from when we grew up. If you are like me, you used to listen for hours to your favourite radio station on a "boombox" so that you could hear your favourite songs. If you wanted to record the song on a cassette tape, without actually having to go the record store and paying for it, you would have to perfectly time when to hit the record button. And when recording, the worst thing was when the DJ would start talking before the song was over! Thursday evenings at 9 pm were reserved for watching television, as that is when my favourite TV shows were scheduled. The only way I could watch *Beverly Hills 90210* or *Seinfeld* was to make sure I was free at that time, or I would miss seeing it—no PVRs or video-on-demand at that time!

No one can argue the fact to be successful in our careers, and every-day life, the ability to use technology is a required skill. It is rare to think of anyone, no matter their age, who hasn't had to adapt to using technology in some way.

Not only do we have more technology available to us today, but we have the ability to connect to the internet, where we have access to an overwhelming volume of information and entertainment at our fingertips. Have you ever thought about listing of all the ways you use technology every day? Here is my list as an example:

- Check my bank account balances online

- Research hotel reviews on TripAdvisor to pick the one to stay at for an upcoming vacation
- Confirm the time of my son's game this Saturday on TeamSnap, the team management app
- Reply to my son's text that he is walking from school to his extracurricular activity
- Review posts from my friends and family on Facebook
- Respond to a former colleague's post on LinkedIn regarding professional networking
- Discover new recipes on Pinterest for what to cook for dinner
- Read an e-book on my tablet

After you create your list, evaluate it. What did you notice after you listed all of the ways you use technology? Are you surprised by how many things you listed? Were there tasks you do that have made your life easier because of improving technology?

I think about the banking example, and how it has evolved even further than getting a debit card and not having to go into a branch to use an ATM to do my banking. Now, I simply "tap" my card as I get my coffee, or pay for my gas or groceries. I use my smartphone to deposit cheques into my account using my mobile banking app. I don't actually remember the last time I went into a bank branch!

Next, I want you to recall something that you did recently using technology that was new to you. For example, we installed a new thermostat that is a computerized "smart device" that allows us to control the temperature of our home. The thermostat is much better than our old manual dial-style one and can let us program a schedule for the temperature we want at different times of the day, and even has the ability to sense when we are home or not and adjust itself accordingly in order to be more efficient. I can also remotely control the temperature from an app on my phone, just in case I forget to turn down the temperature, or if it is too hot in our bedroom at night and I am too lazy to go downstairs to fix it. Every month, I receive an email that gives us data on how much energy we used and how we could become more efficient. It took me relatively no time to learn how to use it, and how to make it work to my advantage.

My point is, when we understand the benefits of technology, we can adapt to using it in our daily lives quickly. Our kids have an ability to learn to use technology that is much faster than most parents. How can you embrace this skill, and benefit from it? Or perhaps you have experienced this firsthand. Have you ever had to teach your parents how to use technology? I recall having to explain to my dad how to use his banking card to pay for groceries. He must have been overwhelmed at this new advancement in banking at first, but it became a part of his regular routine in no time at all.

Think of how the size of computers has changed over the past 20 years. Your first computer was likely a massive box that took up most of the desk and was not portable at all. Today, many of us have smartphones that are really microcomputers that are more powerful than the massive computers we owned previously. Connectivity is instantly accessible, and shared data plans and wifi are ubiquitous.

Setting Limits

With all of this access, another question I get asked is: "Should I limit access to their technology and, if so, what limits do you set?" Although the internet adds another layer of complexity, much of this is probably not too different from what our parents faced in deciding how much TV to let us watch, how much time we could spend on our Ataris, or whether we should be allowed to have our own phone lines in our bedrooms.

One thing to consider is that you can't control all your kid's screen time, especially when your kids are outside of your home. Many use tablets or laptops in their school, where coursework has online components, and they may need to use them to do their homework. My son's school no longer has physical textbooks. Rather, all of his course materials are online, so he needs to use the computer to access it. He submits most of his assignments online through email and Google Drive. It amazes me the work schools are doing with kids online. My son often has to prepare presentations for his coursework, and his slide decks are often better than the ones I have done for work!

The reality is that not all screen time is equal, and we can't limit all of its use. I get that it is hard not to feel guilty when you hear the latest news story or study advising how much screen time is recommended for your child. But for parents of tweens and teens, the recommendations from these studies are vague and just recommend that less time should be spent. Not even the Canadian Paediatric Society has recommended guidelines for children over the age of 5. The US equivalent, the American Academy of Pediatrics, lumps advice for children aged 6 and older. They advise placing limits on the time spent using media and the types of media, and to ensure that it does not take the place of adequate sleep, physical activity, or other healthy behaviours.

What we can learn from this? We need to trust our instincts as parents, and to focus on what we know about what we value. We have to teach our kids how to manage their time and to establish a balance between online activities and encouraging them to do things outside of technology. Encourage them to play a sport, a musical instrument, or an activity in the arts. The benefits of these activities are endless, including the fact that they will learn that they will have to practice to get better and work for what they want in order to succeed.

I like to focus on three things for my son when it comes to his use of technology outside of homework: time, place, and content. I don't mind him watching some YouTube videos to unwind when he comes home from school. How is that any different than what I did when watching some mindless television afterschool. I watched the Young and Restless every day... talk about time wasting! However, he watches these videos while he relaxes on the couch in our living room. I have the benefit of regularly working from home, so I can check in on him and ensure that those few videos don't run on into hours. I can also see what videos he is watching because he uses my login to YouTube on his smartphone. That way, I can see the history of all the videos he watches.

Another thing to consider is: "How do you model using technology to your kids?" I have to use my smartphone and computer for work every day. And, every day I have to catch myself to make sure I am not distracted by using my phone when I am supposed to be spending time with my family. I need to be a good role model for managing the time I spend online. I find this especially challenging because I work from home, as I do not have a typical 8–5 job, Plus, I work in social media for a living, so sometimes the line for balancing home life and work is very blurred.

What limits do you have for yourself regarding technology use? I think that just like anything else in life, it's about discipline and moderation.

If you reflect on how you use technology at home and you are concerned that you might be sending the wrong message, you have an opportunity to teach your kids an important lesson about setting boundaries. If checking your Facebook or Twitter feed is an obsession, find ways to disconnect. If you do not need to know the instant when a message or email arrives, turn off your notifications in the settings of your phone so you are not feeling a constant need to check it.

The reality is that mistakes will be made in this journey. You will make mistakes, and so will your child. The key is how we deal with these mistakes and react to them. I will be addressing some of these potential pitfalls in Chapters 5 and 6.

What is a Social Citizen?

We can't assume that our schools are teaching everything our kids need to know about being good social citizens online. I define a social citizen as a person who develops the knowledge and skills to use social media and other digital media effectively and responsibly. One of the best ways to teach this is to model the behaviour we want to see in our kids ourselves.

In my research for writing this book, I found many parents have the perception that they can't trust their kids with technology or on social media. They let their fears of what they are unfamiliar with take control and affect how they talk to their kids about it. This fear represents another important opportunity for you to be aware of in that your reactions affect how you discuss these things with your kids. If you react negatively, your kids will pick up on that and may avoid talking to you about their concerns or challenges.

This potential lack of communication with your kids could potentially lead to problems if something serious did happen and your child feels like they can't talk to you without an "I told you this would happen" lecture. Strive to remain as neutral as possible with your opinions, and be open-minded.

I also encourage you to make a regular habit of learning more about technology. This may help you build a better relationship with your child, and it may even help you in your own personal and professional life. Actually, I commend you for reading this book as a first step, and I have included other suggestions of websites and books you may want to read the "Resources" section. You can't control everything your child does, online or in their everyday lives offline. But we can set them up for success by teaching them and modelling good habits.

We need to continually help our kids with the challenges they face in managing their time, relationships, and the ability to create, share, and consume content online. These foundational skills are important for both online activities and offline as well.

CHAPTER 3

WHY SOCIAL MEDIA ISN'T AS BAD AS SOME SAY

Here is a headline you won't see very often, but it's true—social media can have positive effects on your teen. I know for some parents this will be an eye opening chapter because often when we think about social media and kids, all of the stereotypical assumptions come up such as kids being obsessed with their devices, that they waste too much time online, and they share way too many selfies.

It would be wrong to assume that what kids are doing online is useless. If you talk to teens about how they use social media, many will tell you that social media has many positive benefits, like being able to connect with friends or being a part of a cause for something they believe in.

I can understand how it is challenging to find the positive in what we may perceive as time wasting or pointless activities online. Let me provide an example of an event that was pivotal in my understanding of how social media can be positive for teens.

In the summer of 2014, I was managing the social media accounts for Travel Alberta, the tourism marketing agency for the Government of Alberta. It was an amazing role and I loved the opportunity to help promote the beauty of my province by sharing photos, videos, and stories of things to do and see online. In tourism marketing, it is common to host media writers on visits to your destination and, in return, they would create news stories that would be seen by the audience of their magazines, newspapers, or TV shows. With the way that people were changing how they learned about new places to visit, there was a rise in the popularity of bloggers, and Travel Alberta was progressive in their thinking by embracing these new media creators.

One visit stands out, in particular. It was when we hosted two YouTube vloggers from the United Kingdom—Ben Brown and Steve Booker. Prior to hearing about these two young men, I had never heard of a vlogger and had no idea what that was. Luckily, a quick search on Google provided me with a better understanding of what they do. A video blog or video log (vlog), is form of blog in which the medium is video, and is actually a form of web television. At the time, Ben Brown was a rising star on YouTube, and he had over 200,000 subscribers to his YouTube channel, where he shared daily videos journaling his activities and life. Many of his videos were watched by over 10,000 people each day, which is a lot of people. At the time of writing, Ben's videos on YouTube were viewed more than 122 million times!

I met Ben and Steve in Jasper, Alberta and I spent the day with them travelling the beautiful Icefields Parkway through the Canadian Rockies on our way to Calgary. If you want to watch the episode on YouTube, it's called *Mind Blowing Views* on his channel, MrBenBrown. On our drive, there were many beautiful viewpoints and we stopped at one at Peyto Lake to take in the scenery. As we walked down the trail, we were approached by a family of four with two very excited teens from London, England. They ran down the trail towards us and, at first I was concerned that maybe they were in a panic to warn us about some wildlife—like a bear—was ahead. But it quickly became clear that the teens had spotted two of their favourite celebrities, Ben and Steve. As they talked excitedly with the guys, I talked to their parents about this random encounter.

The parents told me that their two kids, a son and daughter, loved watching Ben's YouTube videos and were inspired by his positive energy and adventures. After taking some photos together and sharing some of the experiences that the family had enjoyed while on their vacation, they said good-bye. It was amazing to all of us that this chance encounter in the middle of the Canadian Rockies wilderness could happen. If you chose to watch the video, you will see that during the rest of their visit they met up with hundreds of their fans in Calgary, too.

I had no idea that YouTubers were so popular, and as he shared a new vlog every day of his trip I was amazed at the positive comments he would get. Many of his fans said they loved watching his travels and the experiences he shared. They spoke of how they enjoyed learning about other parts of the world and how he created beautiful videos and photography on Instagram.

Since that first visit, I have stayed connected with Ben and Steve through social media. I watch their videos and follow their Instagram accounts (@mrbenbrown and @stevebooker) and love vicariously traveling around the world through them. It is pretty amazing to see to young, talented men do what they love, while living from the content they create on social media.

There are so many teens using social media in positive ways. As parents, we can help guide and even encourage them to use it for good. Here are a few ways social media can be a positive experience for kids.

1. Connection

At the root of social media is the connection that people can have and the ability to communicate with each other using technology. That is the key difference between social media and traditional media (like watching a TV show or a movie)—we can easily engage with others using social media. We are drawn to this ability because humans are social by nature. We seek opportunities to connect with others in real life and online. This helps explain why social media has exploded in popularity in the past decade. We like to connect with our friends and share our personal experiences with one another. Another benefit is for kids who might be shy or who live in an isolated area, as they can connect with others who have common interests. Indeed, there are online groups for almost every interest and hobby in the world, from obscure to very niche.

2. Communication

For some people, it is easier to find their voice and communicate online than it is in person. The ability to think about what you want to say and then type and post it, allows more time to consider your thoughts and feelings. Social media can also provide the opportunity for some people that may be shy to openly discuss their opinions in public and to contribute their opinions on topics that interest them. This can help build their confidence and self-esteem.

The ease of communicating online and using social media allows kids to connect with their friends more often. The benefit of this is that it can help kids learn more about each other and can build trust and strengthen relationships. I have heard of many positive examples of kids using social media to stay connected with friends who no longer go to the same school, or may have moved to another country. Maintaining a friendship online can help bridge the physical distance and allow friends to stay connected. It can also help kids in rural or remote areas feel less isolated.

3. Creativity

The ability to create and share photos and videos has never been easier, and the large volume of content we see daily on social media has expanded our creative horizons. Social media seems to be fueling a creative process and our kids are embracing it. They have the ability to take a photo or video with the camera on their phone, and then add cool edits to those images and videos like text or colors, music, and more. The sheer volume of photos and videos that kids are taking might seem confusing to parents, as there has been a massive shift in consumption from when we grew up! When I was a teen, I was lucky to have a compact camera, but I then needed to buy film, remember to bring the camera to events, take the photo, and then have the film developed. If I wanted to share the photos with friends, I had to have copies made. Back then, we took photos of major life moments, graduation, and other special events, rather than everyday happenings. No wonder some parents are baffled when they see their kids taking what may seem like hundreds of photos each day of what they would never think to take a photo of. It is the idea of capturing and sharing what is happening now, in the moment.

I am often amazed at the creativity that some kids have when sharing videos on YouTube, for example. This ability to create and edit content and be familiar with the process is a skill I think most adults would love to have. I know that in my marketing profession, many businesses pay lots of money to outsource these skills to complete projects. Our kids are gaining skills that may be very helpful in future job market.

4. Confidence

The content that kids share online helps them articulate what they like, what matters to them, and helps to personalize their identity. Whether they post a picture of the sneakers they just bought or a quote that inspires them, each post can create links to others who share that same interest. The comments they get from posting on social can help build confidence and self-esteem. For the most part, comments from friends tend to be positive and provide a degree of validation of their friendship. These comments can also create a sense of community and encouragement that can provide more confidence to pursue interests further.

I have seen this first-hand on Instagram, where I follow many landscape and outdoor photographers. When they share a beautiful photo, I am astounded at the volume of positive comments celebrating the photo, and the talent required to take that photo. I have also been on the receiving side when I have shared a photo and have had people comment positively. It is a nice feeling when people take time to share a positive reaction and can be encouraging to want to share more.

5. Learning

Social media and websites give us instant access to learn about any subject we want to know more about. Information is more accessible than ever before and social media can allow us to share what we know and have learned from others. And, generally, the content is in an engaging format such as videos, which are more interesting to watch than it is to read about. Kids can learn from others, interact, and share ideas online in so many innovative ways that have not been possible before. For example, the ability to talk to an astronaut in space, or connect with a classroom in another country in real time, creates new possibilities for learning. We also have the ability to search for answers online for almost anything we want to learn about. YouTube is the second largest search engine in the world next to Google (who owns YouTube). We can watch videos on anything from how things are made, how to solve complex algebra problems, or learn to play the guitar.

6. Compassion

Social media can help kids who may be feeling lonely or depressed find people to talk to when they are most vulnerable. Lilly Singh, a YouTube celebrity known to her fans as Superwoman, shares videos with empowering messages about overcoming depression, and dealing with life's every day challenges. Videos like hers can make others feel like they are not alone, and provide inspiration to those in need to find help and improve.

Many teens have found their voices online by promoting awareness for a cause they are passionate about and important social issues. Erinne Paisley, a teen from Victoria, British Columbia, used social media to open discussions about causes she believes in. In her book, Can Your Smartphone Change the World? she shares examples of how she felt empowered to use social media as a positive tool. She is best known for her prom dress that was made out of paper, specifically her math homework assignments, which she used to raise awareness about gender equality and education. The dress had the words "I've received my education. Not every woman has that right. Malala.org" written in red ink across the bodice. She donated the money she raised to the Malala Fund, which globally advocates for girls' education.

Hannah Alper, from Toronto, Ontario, is another teen who is using social media for good. She is a blogger and motivational speaker who is passionate about the environment, anti-bullying, and social justice. Her blog, CallMeHannah.ca, shares stories and examples to help inspire other kids to believe that taking small actions can add up—making a difference in the world.

These are some of the benefits of using social media and technology. And the benefits aren't limited to our kids, they can be experienced by people of all ages.

I am very aware that each of these examples can be countered by naysayers with a negative aspect of social media and technology, however, I choose to focus on the positive aspects of social media. Trust me, in a quick Google search you will have no trouble finding articles about the negative aspects, as those headlines can be found everywhere. By reading this book, you have the opportunity to remain open-minded and develop tools to help guide your kids to discover positive uses of technology and beneficial uses of social media.

CHAPTER 4

PLAYING IT SAFE

The internet is a part of everyday life for most children, so it is important to know how to be safe. We need be aware of what our kids are doing online, the content they are watching, who they are communicating with, and what they share about themselves. We should also establish clear boundaries and guidelines for using social media and digital technology, and have frequent discussions with them to ensure we have an active role in their online activities.

Outside of Your Comfort Zone

Social media and technology might seem daunting for some parents. Its use might push you beyond your comfort zone or your own personal beliefs. I want to assure you that you are not alone. There is a very broad spectrum of attitudes and beliefs from parents on this subject. If you can picture a line extending from left to right, at the far left would be parents who are concerned about the effects of technology and the safety risks of being online. Some of these parents believe that the best protection is to keep their kids off the internet for as long as possible.

Moving along the spectrum a little from the left are parents who allow their child to use the internet and digital devices, but with very strict limitations. Often, I will hear parents describe at great lengths how they have set up a monitoring service, or regularly spy on their child's online activity. There are many devices and services on the market for parents that can do everything from blocking inappropriate websites, to setting time limits for wifi access and tracking interactions on social media.

When we gave my son his first smartphone, we had a GPS locating app on his phone that provided a map with his location. It gave me peace of mind knowing that I could go online and see exactly where he was, especially in the time between when school ended and he took the bus ride home. I could track his movement from the bus stop until he walked through the front door, which in reality was only a few blocks. After the first few days of checking in on the app, I noticed I started to use it less and less. I had the security of knowing it was in place if I needed it but, in our case, I haven't used it for quite some time. I was also "that parent" that drove behind the school bus the first time he took the bus in Grade 1, just to make sure he arrived safely. I did it once—okay, maybe twice—and then stopped when I realized he was safe and that it was not an effective use of my time or energy.

To Monitor or Not?

While I respect parents' decisions to do what they feel is necessary to keep their kids safe, I caution parents not to monitor and control all online activity and to not let fear determine your parenting decisions. If it is something you want to do when your child is learning to use technology for the first few months, it makes sense. Another strategy for parents who are open to introducing technology and social media is to limit its use, as a starting point. You can also set the privacy settings so that you can control the experience on certain social media sites such as Instagram, so that you can restrict who can see the content they share and who is allowed to follow their account. As your child demonstrates that they are able to follow your rules and meet your expectations of healthy habits and behaviour, you can determine what you will allow next.

There are lots of apps and devices available for purchase that will monitor your kid's online activity. The features they offer range from the ability to set time restrictions, to limiting what websites they can use. There are, however, potential pitfalls with regards to using parental surveillance apps and devices. If you rely on technology to monitor your kids, you may have a false sense of security. There are many examples of kids figuring out how to disable or bypass these devices and services without their parents knowing. Kids are often smarter than some parents when it comes to technology. The bigger concern that I have is that if we do not support our kids using technology, when something does happen online that makes your child uncomfortable, they may choose not to share it with you out of fear of you getting upset. You do not want your child to hide their online activity from you.

On the other end of the spectrum, at the far right are the parents who are allow their kids to use the internet without any supervision or guidelines. This usage can be more harmful than the good that is intended, because the child will not learn to use the internet safely and may put themselves in risky situations.

Don't Allow Fear to Make Your Decisions

No matter where you are on this spectrum, I think it is important to honestly acknowledge your thoughts and feelings about technology and the internet. Do you assume that the worst can happen if you allow your child to use social media?

Please, don't let fear-based headlines in the media scare you into believing that if you allow your child to use technology in their daily lives, something awful will happen to them. It is very important to realize that the majority of people online are good and will do no harm. It is also realistic that there is an element of society, both online and in our everyday lives, that are bad people. This is a reality that is not new because of the internet, as it is a truth we have had to navigate for generations. Scaring our kids to think that all adults online are bad isn't the right approach.

I am sure you can think of an example from the news of a terrible crime that frightened you, and made you fear if it could happen to you too. For example, I remember back in 1983 when a six-year-old girl from Edmonton went missing. She was supposed to walk home from her elementary school for lunch, and she never arrived. No trace of her has ever been found, and the case of what happened to Tania Murrell remains a mystery. The story of her disappearance made international news and was the headline for many months in our newspaper, in addition to being on the radio and TV news in the Edmonton area. I remember the fear that this instilled in our community, especially since there were no clues and no suspects in the case. I can only imagine how frightened parents must have felt during this time. I also remember being very scared of what if something like that happened to me. For the longest time, I would walk as fast as I could from the bus stop to home. I was a shy girl to begin with, so the added fear of strangers was very real for me.

"Stranger Danger" was a topic that both my school discussed and educated us about. And I remember my parents talking to me about the importance of being aware of my surroundings, and what to do if I ever felt unsafe. They made sure I knew the reality of what the headlines were, but reassured me that this was unlikely to happen to me. They spoke frankly but with reassurance and let me know what to do if I was ever confronted with a difficult situation.

Frightening your child can be paralyzing to both you and your child. Scaring our kids into thinking that the worst can happen if they venture online, or that all adults online are bad, isn't the right approach. It is better to speak openly about safety issues, keeping in mind both the age and maturity of your child.

What You Can Do

Once you determine where you are on the spectrum, I encourage you to increase your knowledge about social media and digital technology use. To help you get started, there are many resources listed on my website socialcitizens.ca. The good news is that you will not need to be an expert, but just need to stay current. I would suggest that you make it a regular habit to stay up to date on the latest apps and sites that your child has access to, or may want to use.

I encourage you to make time to regularly talk with your child about what they do online. Be positive, open-minded, and interested in what they do … without resorting to being judgemental. In our family, I frequently have conversations with my son about what he does on his phone and on the computer.

Here is how I begin conversations:

- I ask questions about what he is doing online. "What videos are you watching? What app do you like using best? Why?"
- Whenever something comes up in the news that is a timely topic, I talk to my son about it. I want him to understand how it affects us, and also to understand that not everything you see in the media or online is completely true.
- I have made sure that my son knows that he can come to me or his dad if he ever encounters something online he is uncomfortable with. He knows that we will not react with anger.

If you encourage an open dialogue and demonstrate that you are interested in what your child is doing online, I believe they are more likely to come to you if they encounter something they are uncomfortable with. For example, a couple of months ago my son came to me about something that upset him. Someone was posting comments on his Instagram account that were negative about him and hurtful. These posts were being made anonymously and he did not know who was responsible, or why they were saying what they had posted.

At first, he was reluctant to tell me about it, but when he opened up and shared with me what was going on, I listened. I did not interrupt, overreact, or delete his Instagram account. Together, we discussed the comments, how they made him feel, and how he should best handle the situation. I told him that in my experience that it was usually best not to respond to online "trolls" and to do his best not to take their negative comments towards him personally. I told him that just like bullies, the behavior and comments that were made, were likely because they were jealous of him and insecure.

I reassured him that the best thing he did during the situation was to come and talk to me, and to vent about how upset he was about it. Heeding my advice, he didn't respond. The good news in this situation was that the troll only posted a couple of more times and then stopped. We would have had to take different action steps if it had not stopped.

The key takeaway is that, because we had an ongoing dialogue about using social media, he came forward to talk to me about the issue. I was familiar with how to best handle a situation like this, and together we came to a conclusion for how he would handle this instance.

Real Dangers Online

I don't want to imply that everything is fine on the internet, and that you don't need to be concerned for the safety of you or your child. You need to be aware about common dangers of being overly exposed online. We have the responsibility as parents and caregivers to keep our children safe from online dangers. So, what are the dangers? And how can you best protect your child from them?

- They may encounter something online that is inappropriate for them to see.
- They may send or be the recipient of photos or videos, including sexting.
- They may encounter bullying or other types of mean online behaviour.

A first step in helping educate your child about online safety is to teach them the importance of protecting your personal information online. A basic rule would be to never share any personal information online. You need to review all of the information that is personal, some examples include:

- Your birthday
- What team(s) you play for
- What school you go to
- Where you live/your address
- Names of family members
- Your email
- Your phone number

Be familiar with the settings on each device you allow your child to use. You can set up parental controls and filters on gaming consoles, smartphones, tablets, computers, and laptops that you may have. These controls are a good idea as they can help reduce the risk of seeing inappropriate content online. You can search online for detailed instructions for your electronic devices to show you how to do this properly. You can also set content filtering options with most home internet providers. Regularly checking the privacy settings on social media sites that you allow is also important because they can often change. These are basic steps in your defense to preventing your private information from being shared online.

Know who your child is friends with on social media sites and establish that you will monitor the use of these sites. One of the rules we have in our home is that my husband and I are allowed to do random checks of my son's social media accounts to see what his activities are, and also to review who he is following, and who is following him. Rather than use this as a negative experience for him, I ask him to show me who he interacts with, and we then discuss how he knows them, whether they go to school with him, play sports with him, etc. If he has accepted a friend request or has a follower that is someone he doesn't know or is an anonymous account, we agree to delete or block that person.

These discussions present important opportunities to have open dialogues with your child about online safety. Your child must understand that the internet is a public space and no matter if they think they are having a private conversation, the reality is that this information can be shared online without their consent and can put their safety at risk.

Resources

There are laws that you need to educate your teen about that affect their online use, and they need to be aware of the legal consequences if they are involved. It is important that you yourself are familiar with the laws in the area that you live. In Canada, this information can be found at cybertip.ca. Another excellent resource that explains the risks by age, what parents need to be aware of, and what they can do is protectkidsonline.ca.

Wise Advice

A friend of mine who is a police officer shared the following advice with me:

> *The biggest point I tell kids is this: when you are texting a person, would you say that to the other person if you were face-to-face? If not, don't text it. Also, don't accept friend requests on any social media from people you have never met in real life. If you have never met them, then you really don't know who they are, so don't let them into your private circle of friends! Because if you do, you are inviting a stranger into your home.*

More recently, I heard a second analogy:

> *We don't teach our kids to drive safely by showing them a video, or not allowing them to get in a car. We teach them how to be safe in vehicles by wearing our seatbelts, following the laws of the road, and helping them learn skills to operate vehicles.*

We teach them how to be a defensive driver so that they can minimize their risk of getting in an accident.

If we compare this example to the digital world, our kids are in vehicles. They are using technology every day. It is up to us to help teach them and help them when they make mistakes, so that they know what to do when they are on their own.

You need to be able to talk openly with your kids, without judgement. I can't stress this enough. It is really important that you have frequent, age-appropriate discussions with your child about what you allow them to do online. Please don't make the assumption that they will be okay and that they understand without you needing to say what is appropriate for them to do and what isn't. The best online protection for your kids' safety is you. Your decision to take an active role in navigating your kids' online activities will be one you will also benefit from.

CHAPTER 5

HOW TO BE(COME) A SOCIAL CITIZEN

What is the definition of a Social Citizen?

1. A Social Citizen is a person who develops the knowledge and skills to use social media effectively and responsibly.
2. To be a good Citizen, you must have respect for yourself and others online and have a positive attitude.
3. You are responsible for your actions online.

You might notice that the emphasis for being a responsible Social Citizen is not on the technology. Instead, the focus is on our character, behaviour, and what it means to be respectful and accountable for ourselves. These skills are important both in the online and offline worlds, and are likely lessons you have been teaching your kids long before technology entered their lives.

When you hear negative news stories about incidents of bullying online or kids posting inappropriate content on social media, the headline will often be about the technology. Here is a recent example of a headline, "Teen Uses Snapchat to Buy and Sell Drugs". The comments that follow the article include many parents saying things like: "Another reason not to let my child use Snapchat!" The problem is not the technology, however, it is not Snapchat's fault that this kid is dealing drugs. It is the actions of the kids who did these things, not the technology or social media. If a child is a bully at school, then it is probably not a stretch to assume that they could be a bully online. The problem can be made worse by using social media as a tool to amplify the bully's message, and this can indeed be a serious issue that needs to be addressed. However, believing that bullying will not happen if you do not allow your child to use social media, is not accurate.

Technology Addiction

There have been many news stories and books focused on addiction to technology. I saw a headline today that read, "Smartphones are like Cocaine to Children". We need to navigate technology use and develop a healthy balance with technology because it is certain that our future will involve using devices online. If your child has previously demonstrated a tendency of addictive behaviour to something, you should be cautious with technology use. I don't think it is fair to generalize and blame the technology for the actions and behaviours of our kids. Though the technology can contribute and amplify the problem, it would be rare if it were the sole cause. Anything that has the ability to reward us has the potential to become addictive. The brain has a reward function that tells us to do more of something, however, it does not have the ability to distinguish what we should do more of and what we should not.

I believe this is why there are so many resources available to parents on topics like how to limit technology and social media use. It is much easier to think that we should eliminate it entirely, than it is to address the real issue of a problem behaviour with your child. Many resources focus on what not to do online and aren't proactive about teaching the importance of being positive, respectful, and responsible.

As I stated earlier, I am not a parenting expert. Nor am I a cyber safety expert or a neuroscientist. However, I research as much as I can and use my common sense to make decisions for my child. I don't get freaked out by the latest article telling me the dangers of using Snapchat or Instagram (or whatever the latest social media app headline of the day is). It is actually pretty rare that it is the app that is the actual problem. The real danger lies in what kids are posting. Are they sharing images that are inappropriate? Are they saying things online that they shouldn't? Are they participating in conversations that are hurtful and mean?

We need to help our kids understand that their actions and behaviours matter, both online and offline. In order for us to be able to teach our kids how to be good Social Citizens, we must set good examples. Here are four things you need to do right now to help be and raise a good social media citizen:

1. Be involved

Ideally, before you give your child any device, you spend time to help them learn the proper way to use it. If you didn't, it's not too late. Talk to them about what they are doing online. Check in with them frequently to discuss what they post about and who they are following—be sure to be positive about your check-in. Don't be on the hunt to find them doing something wrong.

If you decide to let your teen use social media, you can make it a requirement that you will be following their accounts. Or if you have a social media savvy friend or relative, you can ask them to act on your behalf to ensure everything is ok. Be open and honest about what your concerns are if you decide to allow them to use social media and connect with others online.

Teach how to be responsible online and be clear about your expectations for behaviour and actions. Your involvement will be more effective than any parental monitoring app available. Teach them what is right instead of trying to use an app or service to catch them doing something wrong. If you do decide to use a monitoring app or service, I think you should be open with your child that you are using it.

We have a rule in our house that any downloads on any devices require parental permission. We also have every password and username of all approved apps and websites that require logins. I also follow my son on his accounts so that I am aware of anything he posts online.

2. Create boundaries

There is no question that boundaries outlining what your child can and cannot do online need to be established, clearly understood and frequently discussed.

You need to determine what is right for your family. Be very clear about what you expect in terms of acceptable behaviours and actions online and what isn't appropriate.

Here are some suggestions to help you:

- Involve your child in creating the boundaries vs. imposing them. Talk WITH your kids, and LISTEN to their ideas to help establish your family guidelines.
- Screentime: What does balance look like? Are you spending time with friends, going outside, getting good grades? Encourage times when no devices are allowed. For example, at family meals or during family outings. Be sure to stick to this rule and model the behaviour you want to see from your kids.
- Consequences: Are you willing to take their devices away if your boundaries and rules are not followed?
- If your child is having trouble, you may want to establish new boundaries. If you discover your child is being bullied, or is receiving inappropriate messages online, you need to take immediate action. Take the device and limit online access, and explain to your child that it is for their safety. You can then take time to decide how you want to handle future access and seek other resources to help you.
- If your child wants to open an account on a social media site, have them explain to you why they want to use it and what they would use it for. This is a good exercise to help you understand their rationale, and it challenges them to think beyond "just

because their friends are using it".

- Ensure your child has an understanding of the financial aspects of having a smartphone. It is a good idea to explain the costs of a device, how much it costs to replace a screen if it is broken, and how much you pay for data.
- Discuss openly about how much information is too much to share online.
- Most apps, smartphones, and gaming devices all have some form of parental controls and privacy settings. Use them and, if you are unfamiliar, use Google or YouTube to search how set them up properly.
- Be very clear that passwords are private, and that the only people who should share passwords are parents and their child.

It is important to explain, and for your child to understand, that what is shared online can be searched and found by anyone with computer access. Telling them that it could affect their future employment or opportunities to get into advanced education might be too far in their future for them to believe it matters to them, but it could happen. Instead, you could talk to your child about examples of what some people have done online that had negative consequences in order to help educate your child about what happens when you make a mistake online.

Focus on teachable moments rather than lecturing. Try to keep any examples age-appropriate, and continue this conversation throughout their teen years when relevant stories come up in the media. Explain how every email, photo we post, text message we send, or video we share creates data that stays on the internet forever. Teach your child to think twice before they post something. Is this something they want everyone and anyone to see?

Most experts agree that smartphones and other connected devices should not be allowed in the bedroom. There are many reasons to support this recommendation, including the fact that technology keeps us awake and affects our sleep. The choice to shut down your device is a difficult one for most people, including adults. I am guilty of this and, often, the last thing I do before I go to sleep is read my Twitter feed or check the latest updates on Facebook. Or if I wake during the night, I sometimes check my phone and then have difficulties falling back asleep. The temptation to use your device can be hard to overcome, so try leading by example and have your families' devices stay in another room rather than your bedroom.

3. Build trust

Once boundaries are mutually agreed upon, you need allow your kids to explore in a safe way. Part of growing up means kids should be trusted more and rely less on their parents.

It is natural for you to be curious about what your child is doing on the internet. You have the right to monitor your child's phone, but be aware that constant monitoring can cause strain and can be too overbearing. If you are too strict, it can cause your kids to go underground or lie to you, which can happen quite easily. Most kids are better online than we give them credit for.

If you are open and approachable, your child will be more likely to tell you when things go wrong. I want my son to know that he can tell me anything if he becomes uncomfortable about something he sees online, or if his friends encounter something online. If you cannot be open and approachable, make sure that you have an agreement with a trusted adult that they can talk to—this might be a family friend, a relative, a teacher, or a coach.

Let your kids know that if they need help, they can come to you. If they feel threatened or are afraid for their safety, it is important that they talk to you or another trusted adult.

4. Learn together

The debate about banning social media for teens is useless. We are past the point of no return, and social media has now become a part of our daily life. The opportunity is for you to help your kids have a positive experience online.

Apps and new social media channels appear and change daily. It is highly likely your child is more knowledgeable than you are about these new features and ways to use them. Ask your child to show you how they use their apps, and be sure to reserve your judgement of why, and be open to new ways of how kids engage online.

We need to help teach our kids how to respond to different situations online. How not to take things personally, how to remove themselves from an uncomfortable situation, and what they should and should not share online. We will sometimes need to make the decision to make them unplug, to remove themselves from a group, or delete an app.

We need to help our kids evaluate information that they see online in order to determine if it is true. With so much talk about "fake news", we need to encourage our kids to think critically and show them how to research multiple sources of information to find out the truth. One good rule of thumb is that if it sounds too good to be true, it probably is.

It is important that you are aware of any negative effects social media may have on your kids' behaviour. If your son or daughter feels left out or judged by comments made on their posts, or by the number of likes they are getting, you need to intervene and explain that this online value does not equate to the same value in real-life relationships. Teach them the difference between sharing content because they want to versus sharing for acceptance and validation from others.

It is a good idea to share with your child about how you yourself use social media. Do you use it to connect with friends and family? Do you use Pinterest for inspiration and ideas for new recipes to try? If we model ways that we use social media positively, it can demonstrate ways they can use it too.

For example, one way I use social media is to learn new things about social media and digital marketing for my work as a university instructor. I am active on Twitter, and follow many authors and industry leaders I admire. I use Twitter to learn about social media and the constant changes in digital marketing so I can continue to be current with my knowledge for teaching and for my consulting business. My husband uses Twitter to keep current on hockey. He follows players, coaches, agents and media and is up to date on everything to do with a sport he loves. It is a good opportunity to show your teen how social media can connect you to your interests.

Try to make sharing content you see online a part of a regular discussion with your kids. If you see something funny, share it. If you see something that bothers you, discuss it as a family. This will help create an open and ongoing dialogue and will encourage you to share with one another. If you lead, they will be more likely to follow.

I love this example shared by a connection of mine, Shane, on LinkedIn.

My adventure in social media began back in November 2010. I started with Twitter because that was all the rage at the time and I wanted to learn more about social media because my son wanted to open his own social media accounts. I figured I better get ahead of him and learn about this to keep track of him (that only lasts so long). Twitter was very appealing at first, but like most platforms that mature, some of the shine began to wear off after some time. I still use Twitter quite regularly, but I much prefer Instagram.

In March 2013, my son was spending his usual "week on" with me at my house and asked me to open an Instagram account for him. I kind of balked at first but I took him up on his offer. What started out as fun and a way for us to connect turned into an immediate competition for followers. Every other week he'd come back, and we would have to compare our numbers. I had 7 to his 38 in the first week, 13 to his 57 the next week, and this went on and on.

After 1 month, I finally had enough. He left for a week to stay at his mom's and I watched YouTube videos on Instagram. I read articles. I also sent messages to larger profile users and received some responses as to how they grew their followings. So, a week later, my son comes over to my house and immediately after he comes through the door he says, "I'm up to 152 followers dad, how many do you have?"

With a smirk on my face I proudly said, "283 followers". His jaw dropped and his eyes went wide. "Bullshit!" he exclaimed. I handed him my phone "There's no way!" he said. In continued disbelief he dropped my phone and went to his phone to check my profile. It was true; I was way ahead by almost double. He ranted for the remainder of the week and only brought it up occasionally after that.

I waited almost a year to admit to him that I got tired of his cockiness every time he showed up and just bought 250 followers to kick his butt. By then it didn't matter, I had a good understanding of Instagram. My account and followers were growing naturally.

As a parent, you can appreciate how short your time with your children is. My son was gradually moving into his teen years and I just wanted to be able to continue to connect with him and especially make sure he was safe online. He's smart and almost an adult now, so the need isn't as great as it once was, but we've always been close. Now friends, girls, and teenage angst get in the way and Instagram still gives us a way to stay connected. Even though he's grown out of it and moved on to things like Snapchat, he still likes hopping into his dad's posts on occasion.

For me, Instagram is fun. It's my creative release, my daily life online, my photo album to the world. Viewing pictures of faraway places, unique architecture, vacations, inspiring quotes, and more can be fun. You can get lost in it when you need a break from another meeting or a difficult day. You can meet other people from around the world or have a laugh at their latest storyline. You can participate however you want. And sometimes, it's just maintaining a connection with family, in this case, my son.

Your involvement in guiding your kid's digital activity will help them learn what a healthy relationship with digital technology and social media is. We can mentor how to use them respectfully, responsibly, and constructively and to have a balanced approach by modelling the time we spend online and offline.

CHAPTER 6

RESOURCES TO HELP YOU NAVIGATE
THE DIGITAL LANDSCAPE

Visit www.socialcitizens.com for up to date resources.

Throughout this book I have encouraged you to continue your learning of digital technology and social media. To help guide you, I have created a summary of some of my favourite resources. This chapter addresses some of the challenges that you and your child are likely to encounter and how you can navigate them.

I will not attempt to address serious behavioural concerns or issues of internet addiction, cyberbullying, or online safety in this book. If you think that your child may be a victim of these issues, you need to take an active role in the intervention and protection of your child. Get professional help and involve the authorities, as required, immediately!

The reality is that mistakes using technology and social media will happen. How you choose to deal with them and help your child grow and learn is critical. I know this is true in all aspects of parenting, but it is especially important with regards to digital parenting because how you react may impact how your kids make decisions in the future. Try your best to not react solely based on your emotions. Create an environment to have safe, open discussions with your child, and ask lots of questions about what they were thinking when they made the mistake. Teach them about taking responsibility for their choices and actions and how to respond to the seriousness of the situation. Here are some common situations you may encounter:

What if your child has online relationships with people you don't know? Teens use social media to connect and build relationships with people they meet online. Don't assume the worst. Most of these relationships are real and allow our teens to connect with others about common interests. It is very important that you teach your teen about safety concerns and how to recognize when people may not be who they say they are. If your child has a strictly online relationship with someone, ensure that they never agree to meet them without you being present. You may want to implement an agreement that they cannot be connected to anyone they do not (or you do not) know online.

What if your child is being bullied online? Cyberbullying is the term used when someone is bullied online and has received mean or intimidating messages. Unfortunately, digital technology has made bullying more common. It has also increased the awareness among parents and teachers, which can be a good thing. One thing to consider is the degree of the intent of the message. Sometimes, bullying is too broad of a term used when someone says something unkind.

We need to teach our kids what is okay and what is not okay to post online, and to identify what is unkind and mean. This is a good opportunity to discuss with them what they have seen online what they think is not appropriate. For example, what if one of their friends posted a photo of them doing something embarrassing without their permission. How would they feel about that? Talk about the importance of being kind and having empathy about other people's feelings. We also need to teach our kids about the importance of standing up for others when they know someone else is being bullied.

Know the signs of bullying and try to identify them as quickly as possible if you think your child is a victim. A red flag is if you notice your child suddenly becomes anxious or upset when they have been online. If you notice an abnormal change in your child's mood, behaviour, desire to go to school, or time spent with friends or social situations, or if there are complaints of illness, or is developing poor sleep habits, you need to look at the possibility of bullying. If you have any inclination that bullying is happening, discuss this with your child and check their messages and social media accounts. Try to establish what is happening without having any pre-judgement.

What if you think your child is spending too much time online? One of the most important lessons we can teach our kids is about moderation. Kids need to learn how to manage their online presence and their use of digital technology. If you are on your device all of the time, you need to be aware of what you are teaching your kids. You are setting a precedent and modelling behaviour you may not want your child to copy.

If this is a problem for you, you will need to practice not using your devices when you are spending time with your family. Everyone can make the time, even if it is only 60 minutes with no digital distractions once a week. Set guidelines for the amount of time they are allowed to spend online, and how to balance their technology use with other activities. Determine when it is appropriate for them to be online, such as when they are finished their homework, or after they have finished their household chores.

Kids can spend a lot of time online, but if your child is doing well at school, is engaged in other activities like sports or music, and if they have healthy friendships, then you have to trust they are ok and not be too concerned.

What if you discover your child has been on a porn site or a website with inappropriate content? Don't be naive to think that your child will not see content that might be sexually explicit online. Parental controls and filters can help, however if your teen has data on their smartphone, they can be easily bypassed. Your child will eventually need to have the self-control and judgement to manage their actions online—without filters.

Involve yourself in educating your child how to manage the freedom to explore all realms of content online. You need to think about how you will handle it if your child does something online that you do not approve of, before it happens, so that you can be prepared with your response. As an example, if discover your child was on an inappropriate site that was intended for adults, you may want to have an open discussion with them that is age-appropriate for their maturity level.

Acknowledge that it is easy to find content like what they saw, but that they are not old enough to go to sites like that, and that you will be closely monitoring what they view. Most kids are curious and don't want to ask their parents questions, but try to keep the lines of communication open about their sexuality. Try not to freak out, don't get mad at your child, and explain it to help them understand that what they saw can be confusing or even upsetting. Give your child the opportunity to tell you how they feel about seeing that content.

Obviously, this conversation is dependent on the age and maturity of your child. If your child is older, there is a chance that they were searching for this type of content. It is totally natural for kids to be curious and it is your choice how you choose to share your opinion on this topic with your child.

If your child posts something wrong, how can they turn that situation around? Mistakes will be made. Teaching that they need to take accountability, encouraging them to delete the post, and offering a sincere apology to the person offended are good life lessons.

The following are social media sites and websites that are age-appropriate for your child, where you can get reviews of various topics:
*   commonsensemedia.org is one of my favourite resources online. It offers reviews that provide easy-to-understand and

non-technical advice that is age-appropriate too.

- esrb.org the Entertainment Software Ratings Board rates content in video games and apps on age-appropriateness, content, and interactive elements.
- beinternetawesome.withgoogle.com is Google's resource for online safety and digital citizenship.
- microsoft.com/about/philanthropies/youthspark/ youthsparkhub/programs/onlinesafety is Microsoft's resource for online safety for families.
- help.instagram.com is Instagrams' Help Centre, which provides information on setting account privacy and online safety tips.
- snapchat.com/safety is Snapchats' Safety Centre, which also provides information on settings and online safety.

If you are going to let your child use social media such as Instagram or Snapchat under the age of 13, here are a few more suggestions:

- Do not allow them to set-up the account on their own. You need to control the set-up so you know the account login and password.
- Explain the importance of never sharing the password with anyone else.
- Set the account to private. This means you can control who is allowed to follow and see the posts in the account.
- Be clear about the ground rules for posting photos, videos, and messages. No private information can be shared—ever. Discuss what is not appropriate to post, including any content you might not be comfortable with (selfies, certain clothing such as bathing suits, etc.)
- If you are on that social media site, make it a requirement that you follow their account … and that they can't block you!
- Teach about sharing photos: how to take your own and use filters to make your photos better. Also discuss the fact that

you cannot share others' photos without their permission or without tagging them (i.e., giving credit to the original creator).

CONCLUSION

I hope that you have found value in reading this book. My goal was to provide you with a balanced perspective, one that emphasizes a positive approach for how to navigate the digital landscape with your kids. I want you to feel empowered, now that you have more information and the confidence that you can figure this out. You can be an advocate for your child and teach them how to be accountable, responsible, safe, and positive online.

The concerns you have now, will soon be replaced with new concerns about technology that is emerging, such as augmented reality, artificial intelligence, and many other innovations. The opportunities your children will have to learn and benefit from using this technology is unfathomable.

The most important thing I want you to take away from this book is that the use of social media and technology can be a very positive experience. I have made it my career to teach people how to figure out their "a-ha moment" of what they like about being online. What I've found is that there isn't one single approach that works for everyone, and the same will be true for you and your child.

I invite you to continue your learning online with me. My goal is to build a hub of resources for parents and teachers that will help you have better conversations with your kids about technology and social media. I encourage you to follow my blog at socialcitizens.ca for articles about the latest information, and will not condemn technology. In my podcast on Google Play, Stitcher, and iTunes you will hear from experts from around the world about digital citizenship. Or, you can learn more from taking one of my online courses on topics ranging from how to use social media to how to have better conversations with your kids about their online activities.

Together, we can become good Social Citizens.

ACKNOWLEDGEMENTS

I am fortunate to have had a community of friends and family that have supported me in my Social Citizens project.

Alana, Alice, Amanda, Andrew, Anne, Annette, Barbara, Brenda, Cate, Carmen, Caroline, Cassandra, Chelsea, Christie, Darlene, Danielle, Dianna, Don, Doug, Ernest, Evan, Heather, Ian, Jaie, James, Jane, Janice, Jasmine, Jeannine, Jeff, Jennifer, Jeremy, Jess, Jocelyn, Jodi, Jody, Johnny, Jolanda, Judith, Judy, Julia, Julie, Kate, Karen, Kayley, Ken, Laura, Leigh, Lindsay, Lisa, Marilyn, Mary Ann, Marge, Marney, Maureen, Melanie, Michelle, Mindy, Natasha, Nicole, Niesa, Nolwenn, Patricia, Paul, Pola, Rebecca, Reid, Rita, Robin, Sarah, Sean, Shane, Shannon, Shelly, Sherry, Sonja, Stan, Stephanie, Stewart, Sydony, Tania, Taylor, Todd, Tracy, Trish, Veronica, Vince, Warren, Zanette (I apologize if I missed someone!) I want you ALL to know I value and appreciate all that you do for me, and the support you have shown me.

Thank yous also need to go to Calvin Simpson and John McDonald with Happful.com for their support and guidance. Your coaching and willingness to help me actually enjoy the process of writing will forever be appreciated.

Made in the USA
San Bernardino, CA
23 January 2018